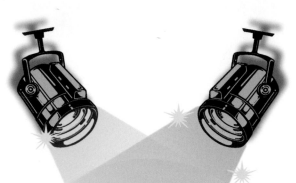

LATINOS
IN THE
LIMELIGHT

Christina Aguilera

Antonio Banderas

Jeff Bezos

Oscar De La Hoya

Cameron Diaz

Scott Gomez

Salma Hayek

Enrique Iglesias

John Leguizamo

Jennifer Lopez

Ricky Martin

Pedro Martinez

Freddie Prinze Jr.

Carlos Santana

Selena

Sammy Sosa

CHELSEA HOUSE PUBLISHERS

LATINOS
IN THE
LIMELIGHT

Jennifer Lopez

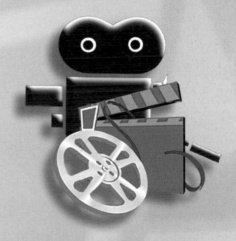

Leah Furman

CHELSEA HOUSE PUBLISHERS
Philadelphia

Frontis: *Actress, singer, dancer Jennifer Lopez flashes her dazzling smile. Her award-winning performances in both films and music have made her a Latina superstar.*

Produced by
21st Century Publishing and Communications, Inc.
New York, New York
http://www.21cpc.com

CHELSEA HOUSE PUBLISHERS

Editor in Chief: Sally Cheney
Production Manager: Pamela Loos
Art Director: Sara Davis
Director of Photography: Judy L. Hasday
Managing Editor: James D. Gallagher
Senior Production Editor: J. Christopher Higgins
Publishing Coordinator: James McAvoy
Project Editor: Anne Hill

The Chelsea House World Wide Web address is
http://www.chelseahouse.com

3 5 7 9 8 6 4

Library of Congress Cataloging-in-Publication Data

Furman, Leah.
  Jennifer Lopez / Leah Furman.
    p. cm. – (Latinos in the limelight)
  Includes bibliographical references and index.
  ISBN 0-7910-6110-8 — ISBN 0-7910-6111-6 (pbk.)
    1. Lopez, Jennifer, 1970–Juvenile literature. 2. Actors—United States
Biography—Juvenile literature. 3. Singers—United States—Biography—
Juvenile literature. 4. Hispanic American actors—United States—
Biography—Juvenile literature. 5. Hispanic American singers—United
States—Biography— Juvenile literature. [1. Lopez, Jennifer, 1970- .
2. Actors and actresses. 3. Singers. 4. Women—Biography. 5. Puerto Ricans—
Biography.] I. Title. II. Series.

PN2287.L634 F87 2000
791.43'028'092—dc21
[B]   00—058531
                                                                 CIP
                                                                 AC

CONTENTS

CHAPTER 1
LIFE IMITATES ART   7

CHAPTER 2
A BRONX TALE   15

CHAPTER 3
DANCING GIRL   21

CHAPTER 4
HOORAY FOR HOLLYWOOD!   27

CHAPTER 5
REACHING NEW HEIGHTS   37

CHAPTER 6
QUEEN OF ALL MEDIA   51

CHRONOLOGY   60
ACCOMPLISHMENTS   61
AWARDS   62
FURTHER READING   62
INDEX   63

LIFE IMITATES ART

Jennifer Lopez first became a household name in 1997 when her celebrated face, and even more celebrated form, graced the cover of countless magazines, appeared in CD store windows, and was displayed on cineplex marquees. A person would be hard-pressed to spend even a day without hearing something or other about this multitalented performer. Jennifer's climb to superstardom is a testament to her ambition and ability, but none of it could have been possible without the film that helped this budding actress turn the corner once and for all.

The film that brought Jennifer out of the shadows and into the limelight was not what anyone would call a big-budget blockbuster. *Selena*, the story of the Mexican-American Tejano singer who rose to unprecedented fame before being fatally shot by the president of her fan club, was made for $20 million and earned a respectable $35 million. The fact that it did not break any box office records mattered little to the millions who flocked to see

---

Playing the role of the beloved Tejano singer Selena, Jennifer gave an exuberant performance. Although Jennifer had appeared in television and films in the early 1990s, it was the 1997 film Selena *that thrust her into the limelight and put her on the road to stardom.*

Critics and fans alike were won over by Jennifer's charm and versatility. Her determination to play Selena and the energy she brought to the role helped make the movie popular.

the biopic of the late, great Latina role model. Besides commemorating the life of one inspirational woman, *Selena* also gave the world Jennifer Lopez. This young acting, singing, and dancing triple threat would do as much as her on-screen alter ego to further the cause of Latinos nationwide.

Before *Selena* and despite a list of film credits, including her starring role in the just released *Anaconda*, Jennifer still did not have that breakthrough role that would make the public stand up and take notice. What thrust her onto Hollywood's most-wanted list was *Selena*. In the title role of Selena Quintanilla Perez, Jennifer stole the show as well as the hearts of theatergoers everywhere.

Film critics were not immune to Jennifer's many charms either. "The teenage and adult Selena is played by Lopez in a star-making performance," raved Roger Ebert of the *Chicago Sun-Times*. "Selena succeeds, through Lopez's performance, in evoking the magic of a sweet and talented young woman." Other reviewers only echoed the above sentiment. "Lopez . . . gives a feisty, buoyant performance that could set her on a star path similar to the singer's," wrote *Time* magazine's Richard Corliss. The *Washington Post's* Richard Harrington was enamored of Jennifer, stating that "the film rightfully belongs to Jennifer Lopez, who captures Selena's luminous beauty, innate sweetness, and boundless energy."

Selena had indeed created a first-rate movie star. Jennifer could not let the film take all the credit for her success, however. As she told the *Toronto Sun*, "I think *Selena* really got my name out there, but Jennifer Lopez didn't do a bad job of that, either."

In fact, Jennifer had to overcome quite a few obstacles just to get the part of Selena. The film, which documented the true story of the singer's rise to stardom and her shocking death, was executive produced by Selena's father, Abraham Quintanilla Jr. His expressed intention was to commemorate the life of his daughter and give her fans a deeply personal portrait by which to remember their hero. With Selena's father at the helm of the production, whoever got the role had to embody the essential quality that made Selena so important to her vast following.

First, Abraham Quintanilla hired Gregory Nava, the director of such lauded Latino films as 1995's *My Family/Mi Familia* and 1983's *El Norte*, to direct and cowrite the story. Then the casting crusade swung into high gear. The team put out a casting call that reached the ears of some 22,000 would-be Selenas, all of whom showed up at audition sites in California, Texas, Illinois, and Florida. Although most of the contenders were amateurs, some professionals also auditioned for the role. Jennifer was one of them.

Having worked with director Nava on *My Family/Mi Familia*, Jennifer knew that she had the inside track when her agent told her about the audition. What she did not know, however, was how badly she would end up wanting the role. After reading the script, Jennifer quickly realized the kind of character she would be dealing with. "Selena was a spirit," she told *Cosmopolitan*. "Nothing was going to stop her. And I admire that kind of drive."

This very drive probably motivated Jennifer during the audition process. Grueling as it was, the audition was no match for Jennifer's unflagging stamina and dancer's physique. She won the part and began earning her $1 million fee, the highest ever bestowed upon a Latina actress at the time. For the former dancer, the part was a natural fit. While growing up and aspiring to Broadway fame, Jennifer had danced and sung in musical theater. Her voice was strong, her moves were sharp, and her star power was as bright as that of Selena herself. Despite Jennifer's talents and film experience and the fact that Nava had worked with her before, he did expect her to submit to several rigorous auditions. In one day, the actress had to perform two of Selena's songs as if she were the late songstress herself and also act in a whopping five scenes. The entire audition took no less than 11 hours. As far as Jennifer was concerned, this was the single toughest test of her career.

But dancing and singing ability alone did not account for Jennifer's success. Her keen understanding of the film's intentions played a significant part in her triumphant audition. Jennifer knew that playing Selena had to be about staying true to the character, as opposed to indulging her own need for artistic expression.

To accomplish this formidable feat, Jennifer did her research. She studied the Tejano star's dialect, gestures, and signature dance moves. She also moved in with Selena's sister, Suzette, and interacted with the Quintanilla family as much as possible. Right from the start, it had been obvious that Jennifer had a great deal in common with Selena. The fact that the two women's values and ambition were an exact match was apparent to both the Quintanilla family and the film's director. The more the Quintanillas discovered about Jennifer, the more their confidence in her ability to portray Selena increased. Not only did Jennifer resemble Selena in personality, mannerisms, and appearance, she even shared some of Selena's bad habits, such as eating junk food. "[Selena's mother] told me I was just like Selena," the actress enthused to *Time* magazine, obviously flattered by the compliment.

Although the Mexican-American community had some reservations about an actress with a Puerto Rican background playing the role of their beloved hero, the sight of Jennifer looking every inch the Tejano sensation pacified any disbelievers. From the color of her nail polish to the tight fit of her clothes to the ring of her laugh, Jennifer brought Selena back to life.

With the final approval of the Quintanilla family, Jennifer knew that her portrayal of Selena could not fail to meet with critical and popular success. She was right. Her performance earned her nominations for a Golden Globe Award for Best Actress in a Comedy or Musical Motion Picture and an MTV Movie Award for Best Breakthrough Performance, as well as a trophy from the American Latino Media Arts (ALMA) Awards for Outstanding Actress in a Motion Picture. Jennifer finally got to walk the elusive red carpet, feel the blinding flashes of hundreds of high-powered cameras, and field scores of questions from reporters. She had arrived.

Jennifer was never a complacent young woman, however. She conquered the world of motion pictures, scoring a $2 million salary, an unheard-of sum for a Latina actress, when she appeared in the film *Out of Sight* in 1998. Following the film, she then refocused her energies on the music industry. As if possessed by the spirit of the slain superstar, Jennifer felt compelled to pick up Selena's torch and run with it. "[W]hen I did *Selena* I realized how much I missed singing and dancing," she explained. "Its just something I always wanted to do. I don't know about conquering the music market, I just want to make a song that everyone sings along to. I don't want to look back and see that I didn't even try when I had the opportunity."

By now the public knows exactly how Jennifer's bid for pop music stardom turned

*Jennifer shows off her
1998 ALMA award as
Outstanding Actress
for her role as Selena.
With this award and
others she won for the
film, Jennifer felt like
she had arrived as a
film star.*

out. Just two years after *Selena* debuted in the theaters, "If You Had My Love," the first single from Jennifer's debut album, *On the 6*, appeared on radio and MTV. The response to the upbeat track was phenomenal, catapulting the new recording artist to the heights of celebrity. Jennifer Lopez had succeeded in continuing Selena's legacy into the new millennium, opening a whole new world not only to Latinos but to people everywhere.

2

A BRONX TALE

Jennifer Lopez was not kidding when she told *Honey* magazine that she "was dancing probably out of the womb." In fact, she does not remember a time when she wanted to do anything other than perform. Her Puerto Rican parents, however, had other plans for the second of their three daughters. The Lopezes oldest daughter, Leslie, was born in 1967, while Jennifer came into the world on July 24, 1970. Lynda came along a year later.

Living in New York's tough South Bronx neighborhood, David and Guadalupe "Lupe" Lopez always believed that great things were in store for their fiery and determined middle daughter. "My parents said that I could do anything even though we were from where we were from and we were who we were as far as nationality went," Jennifer explained. "They taught me that none of that mattered, you know, that we were just as beautiful and smart and intelligent and could accomplish the same things as anybody else in this country."

The only problem was that David's and Lupe's idea of greatness for Jennifer was going to law school and becoming

Jennifer often returns to her roots in New York City's South Bronx community to visit and shop. As she grew up, she was encouraged by her mother to appreciate music and the theater, which inspired young Jennifer to dream of a future as a performer.

distinguished in that profession. While this idea often conflicted with their daughter's determination to become an entertainer, they did indulge her passion for dancing. At the age of seven, they enrolled the little girl in dance classes, and soon she was taking lessons in jazz, piano, and theater.

Although the family lived in a working-class area that boasted more gangs and housing projects than million-dollar homes and tree-lined streets, the Lopez children were not under-privileged. While the first few years of her life were spent in what Jennifer described as "a small apartment that was cold in the winter and hot in the summer," the family's financial outlook soon improved. David Lopez began a steady job as a computer specialist at an insurance company, and Guadalupe became a kindergarten teacher at the Holy Family Catholic School. The Lopezes were soon able to afford a single-family home.

According to Jennifer, the horror stories about her neighborhood have been greatly exaggerated. She does not see The Bronx as a war zone but simply an inner city neighbor-hood like those in many other cities. The area was rough around the edges, but Jennifer quickly learned to appreciate the benefits of growing up a city kid. "I have a lot of street smarts because of the neighborhood I grew up in," she said. "It wasn't so much a bad neighborhood as one where you had to be careful. And the sensibilities you grow up with in a city teach you to be more alert, aware, more careful."

Leslie, Jennifer, and Lynda Lopez came of age just across the street from the Holy Family Church, sharing family life in a comfortable, two-story house with a wood and brick exterior.

The three sisters had some of the best times of their lives playing together. One of the things that they bonded over was their intense love for the same television show—*Charlie's Angels*. "When we would play, I was always Jaclyn Smith," Lynda told *People* magazine. "Leslie was Kate Jackson. Jen was whoever the blonde was—Farrah or Cheryl Ladd."

While Lynda, Jennifer, and Leslie may have played Angels, they didn't always act angelic. Their legendary arguments bore a stronger resemblance to the gang violence depicted in their favorite film, *West Side Story*. Like many siblings who can often be found at each other's throats, the fights between Jennifer and Leslie would start small and end by waking the entire neighborhood. One time, an adolescent Jennifer even chased Leslie around the house with a knife.

Thanks to Lupe's strong influence, musicals became a favorite family pastime. Having tried and failed to become an actress, the girls' mother wanted to develop an appreciation for the arts in her children. "I made my three daughters watch musical films like *West Side Story*," she recalled. "'Sit and watch,' I told them, and they did."

Young Jennifer was only too happy to obey her mother. The young girl loved *West Side Story* right away. Focusing on the struggles of the Puerto Rican community and featuring real Latinos such as Rita Moreno in principal roles, the film inspired Jennifer to shoot for the stars. "There were zero Latinos on TV," she told *People*, "so Rita

Moreno was the only one I identified with."

At school Jennifer sometimes didn't fit in, but she stood up for herself. Demanding respect even as a fourth grader, she got into a fistfight with a friend who had been talking behind her back. Needless to say, Jennifer never had to fight again. According to Jennifer, she knocked down her opponent and won the fight. She has said that she is not proud of what she did but that she made her point. No one bothered her again and she eventually graduated from school without any trouble.

Lupe Lopez's strict parenting had a great deal to do with Jennifer's successful transition from the Bronx to the big time. The concerned mother was convinced that as an early bloomer, Jennifer was in serious danger of winding up an unwed mother. Seeing the potential hazard, Lupe instructed her daughter to dress as conservatively as possible and to stay away from makeup. "My mother used to say, 'I'm so worried about Jennifer because she's so sexy. I'm afraid she's going to get pregnant,'" Jennifer later recalled. "The taste in my neighborhood was for voluptuous women, see? I knew guys liked me."

Taking her mother's good advice to heart, Jennifer kept to the straight and narrow, never picking up the habits favored by so many of her peers, such as smoking, drinking, and drugs. "I was never naughty," she said, "but I was a tomboy and very athletic. I'd always be running around and playing sports and stuff. But I was a good kid. I was always hugging people. I was very close to my grandparents and I listened to my mother and didn't do bad things."

Even when Jennifer was 15 and started to date her first boyfriend, David Cruz, she still

followed her mother's orders. Jennifer and David Cruz would remain an item for nearly nine years before Jennifer's stardom finally put an end to the relationship with her high school sweetheart.

How, though, did she suddenly become a star? Jennifer's big break into show business came as a direct result of her first love, a pursuit that no one had really believed would ever pan out—dancing.

Actress Rita Moreno dances in a scene from the musical West Side Story. *One of the few Latina stars in films at that time, Moreno was a role model for young Jennifer, who was determined that she too would dance and sing one day.*

3

DANCING GIRL

Throughout her school years, there was little to suggest that Jennifer would become one of the most recognizable faces in the entertainment industry. Her family and friends knew she was sweet and dedicated, but she was hardly a trendsetter. She hung around with the drama crowd but was not the star of every high school play. While the fame would come later, Jennifer expressed stage presence from day one. A friend recalled that in one school production of *My Fair Lady*, Jennifer played a poor kid. She was hardly the star, but her friend remembers that she was the one who stood out.

Eventually, however, Jennifer earned a reputation as one of the best dancers at Preston High. She choreographed routines and danced in such school productions as *The Pirates of Penzance* and *Godspell*. "I think that was always her calling," attested Stephanie Halore, Jennifer's high school friend. "She wanted to dance."

Continuing weekly lessons with her sisters, she performed in local dance recitals and also went out for

---

The bright lights of Manhattan lured Jennifer from her home in the Bronx when she knew she had to pursue her love of, and talent for, dancing. She traveled into Manhattan for dance lessons and endless auditions on Broadway until she got her break and began her career as a performer.

auditions. Whether trying out for a school play or something even bigger today, Jennifer always takes rejection in stride, and she strongly believes that her determination in the face of failure is responsible for her success. Jennifer recalls that her older sister, Leslie, who was very talented, could not take rejection. For Jennifer, it was a question of persisting until someone recognized your talent and gave you the opportunity to shine.

Star glow alone does not win auditions, though. Jennifer had to work long and hard to perfect her craft. Despite her parents' plans for her higher education, the young hopeful was consumed by the idea of dancing professionally. One time, when she was just 14, her dance teacher saw her struggling and looking upset in class. Thinking there was probably only one reason why a girl that age would become so miserable, he asked her whether she was having boy problems. He was way off base. "I remember telling my teacher, 'I just want to be better,'" Jennifer said. "And he goes, 'You will.'"

In 1987, when Jennifer graduated from high school, her parents were just as determined to send her to college as she was to embark upon her dancing career. Finally, she gave in and enrolled at New York City's Baruch College. She lasted only one semester before she decided to give it all up for her chance at stardom. Surrounded by the energy and stimulation of Manhattan, Jennifer felt her ambition soar. She was going to dance, and she was going to do it while she was still young enough to succeed. When she broke the news to her parents, they were crestfallen. "When I told my parents I wasn't going to college and law school which was aiming really high where

I came from, but it was an attainable goal—they thought it was really stupid to go off and try to be a movie star," she explained. "No Latinas did that—it was just this stupid, foolish, crapshoot idea to my parents and to everybody who knew me. It was a fight from the beginning."

To pursue her passion, Jennifer rode the subway from the Bronx to Manhattan to take ballet and jazz dance classes. She also began auditioning for countless Broadway musicals and even got a job touring Europe with a variety show called *The Golden Musicals of Broadway*. Despite this success, and the five months of steady pay that it afforded, Jennifer struggled to make ends meet. Fortunately, she was not a young woman who could be scared off by financial difficulties. She was not about to sacrifice her ambitions just to have money to fall back on. Jennifer firmly believed that she had no alternative but to pursue her dream.

By 1989, Jennifer's motivation had begun to pay off. With the whole country suddenly caught up in the heat of the rap explosion, Jennifer's slick, hip-hop moves won her a lot of admirers in the dance community. "Hammer came out with 'U Can't Touch This,' and all the auditions started becoming hip-hop auditions," Jennifer recalled. "I was good at it, and they were like, 'Ooh, a lightskinned girl who can do that. Great, let's hire her!'"

Although she was busier than ever, the young dancer still was not making enough money to support herself. Sometimes, she had to make the $50 that she got for dancing in a music video last an entire month. It was not an easy feat for a natural-born dancer surrounded on all sides by temptations such as New York City's Palladium and Danceteria discos. "There

Keenan Ivory Wayans (center) is surrounded by the Fly Girls from his television show In Living Color. *As one of the Fly Girls, Jennifer (standing at left, leaning on Wayans's shoulder) moved to Los Angeles, the heart of the entertainment industry.*

were times when I was really down to my last dollar," she recalled. "And then my last 50 cents . . . and then my last quarter."

Like so many young dancers who flock to New York to seek their fortunes, Jennifer could have used her talent and looks to get a job as a go-go dancer. Such a move would have been easy, but Jennifer thought better of it. To her, go-go dancing was just a trap. She would not get sidetracked, even if it meant making hundreds of dollars a night. Instead, she kept her eye on the future—and prayed for a miracle. In 1991, Jennifer's prayers were finally answered.

It happened during an open call for the Fox network's sketch-comedy series *In Living Color*. As Jennifer was sweating her heart out alongside 2,000 other trained dancers, choreographer Rosie Perez picked her out of the line. "There was just an unshakable confidence about Jennifer," Eric Gold, the series coproducer who would eventually become Jennifer's manager, recalled. "No doubt, no fear. The girl just had it."

Jennifer's first big break was the one she needed to start her career. As one of the show's Fly Girls, she performed the pulse-quickening dance numbers between sketches. Since the show featured such Los Angeles-based stars as Jim Carrey and the Wayans Brothers, Jennifer had to pack her bags and relocate to Los Angeles.

4

HOORAY FOR HOLLYWOOD!

For the first time in her life, Jennifer had something to show for all her hopes, dreams, and ambition. Dancing on *In Living Color* paid very well and only required her to work one day a week. The rest of the time she was free to take acting classes and spend time with David Cruz, who had followed her to California. According to the show's makeup artist, David "seemed so sweet but not quite ready for prime time, like the high school boyfriend who was going to get left behind."

Jennifer's career began to pick up speed. The acting classes soon yielded results—the first of which was to make the dancer dream of life beyond her leotard and dance tights. Jennifer had already tried her hand at acting, auditioning for a series of television commercials in New York, but she had never thought she could be good at it. However, having discovered this new way to show her talent, Jennifer wanted nothing so much as to doff her dancing shoes and sink her teeth into a meaty, dramatic role.

For a young hopeful, Hollywood was the place to be, and Jennifer was soon recognized and tapped for roles in several television series. But feature films were her goal, and endless auditions and her own confidence and determination began landing her roles on the big screen.

It seemed as if Jennifer had only to take some classes and a lucky break would materialize out of nowhere. One day, some two years into her stint on *In Living Color*, Jennifer received an offer to play a recurring role on the Fox television series *South Central*. The husband of another Fly Girl was producing the program and decided to cast Jennifer after seeing her dance on the show. Jennifer won the role of Lucy, but *South Central* was soon cancelled because of low ratings.

Fortunately for Jennifer, the show did bring offers for more TV shows, and she auditioned every chance she got. Eric Gold, who had become her manager, vowed to make her a star like his other client Jim Carrey, also a performer on *In Living Color*. True to his vow, Gold soon led Jennifer to more television jobs. She appeared as Melinda Lopez on the short-lived CBS series *Second Chances* in 1993. When that show died, her character was spun off into another flash-in-the-pan series called *Hotel Malibu* in 1994. Between those two series, Jennifer also found time to play the role of Rosie in the made-for-television movie *Nurses on the Line: The Crash of Flight 7*.

Despite her promising career in television, Jennifer still wanted to break into feature films. Rejecting television offers for big-screen prospects, she auditioned time after time. She finally got her shot when director Gregory Nava cast her in his epic *My Family/Mi Familia*. The story, which focused on three generations of one Mexican family, featured Jennifer as the young Maria, the matriarch of a family that emigrates to California from Mexico in the 1920s. In the role of Maria, Jennifer showcased the full range of her talent by acting in a variety

of dramatic scenes. While the film did not score big at the box office, the actress's considerable abilities were noticed by Nava. He praised her as "beautiful and phenomenally gifted."

Such positive affirmation clearly strengthened Jennifer's resolve and self-confidence. Soon after the movie wrapped, she was back auditioning for different film roles. Wherever she tried out and no matter which director she read for, Jennifer was always sure of one thing—an audition was her place to shine. Crediting her attitude with her fame, she has described her audition strategy:

> [E]ach day I had an audition, I'd wake up, do my hair and my makeup, look at myself in the mirror and say, "I have the stardom

In scenes like this one from her first feature film, My Family / Mi Familia, *Jennifer proved her range of acting talents. Jennifer's highly praised performance earned her more film offers, which showcased her versatility as an actress and increased her opportunities to play major roles.*

glow today." A lot of people go into meetings and auditions all nervous. No! You've got to have WOW! I tell my actress friends this all the time. I walk into auditions going, "What's gonna make me different from all the other girls here?" They're looking for the next star to walk into that room. It's about being alive, open, electric, confident. That's the "wow."

Soon, Jennifer's "wow" landed her in another feature film, one that handed her a higher-profile part. Even Jennifer could hardly believe her luck in being cast as Grace Santiago, the female protagonist in *Money Train*. Not only was Grace both Wesley Snipes's and Woody Harrelson's love interest, she was also a tough New York City transit cop who takes on Snipes's character in a kickboxing match. That staged bout between Wesley and Jennifer must have been somewhat cathartic for the actress. A few years after completing the movie, she went on record to say that she had had a hard time fending off Snipes's advances during filming. "He got really upset about it," Jennifer revealed. "His ego was totally bruised. He wouldn't talk to me for two months. . . . Actors are used to getting their way and to treating women like objects." With David Cruz still very much in the picture, Jennifer had no intention of dating anyone else.

For Cruz, however, the view from Hollywood was altogether different. Love scenes were a part of the business, but watching his girlfriend get romantic with other men, especially rich and famous movie stars, bothered the somewhat traditional Cruz. Other problems cropped up as well. As an up-and-coming actress, Jennifer was always working, striving, and planning.

Whereas her attempts invariably met with success, Cruz found it hard to make his way in Los Angeles. Finally, both admitted that their long-term relationship had hit a brick wall. Jennifer has explained, "Career-wise, we weren't in the same place. He just didn't know what he wanted to do. . . . I was so fast. I was like a rocket, he was like a rock."

Although the breakup was no doubt painful to Jennifer, she accepted it as inevitable and continued to pursue her acting career. Despite the lackluster reception of *Money Train*, Jennifer's career was still going strong. Even those critics who had nothing nice to say about the film itself reserved some praise for Jennifer's performance. As Hal Hinson wrote in the *Washington Post*, "To further complicate matters, the filmmakers provide a love interest—a gorgeous transit cop

Jennifer appears in a scene from Money Train *with costars Wesley Snipes (left) and Woody Harrelson (center). Although not a huge hit, the film was a success for Jennifer, who received good reviews for her performance and attracted the attention of a major director, Francis Ford Coppola.*

played gracefully by Jennifer Lopez—who pits the brothers against each other."

Thanks to the talent that won her glowing reviews, Jennifer soon returned to face the camera. To her amazement, her work in *My Family/Mi Familia* and *Money Train* had inspired the confidence of five-time Academy Award-winning director Francis Ford Coppola. Convinced of Jennifer's talent, the director hired her to take a key supporting role in his film *Jack*. The film starred Robin Williams as a 10-year-old boy with a rare aging disorder that makes him look like he's 40. Jennifer played Jack's fifth-grade teacher and the object of his schoolboy affection.

Working on the movie was an extremely rewarding experience for Jennifer. Having only the small budget *My Family/Mi Familia* and the poorly received *Money Train* under her belt, the opportunity to collaborate with people like Francis Ford Coppola and Robin Williams was almost too good to be believed. Best of all, Coppola was generous enough to invite the entire cast to his Napa Valley estate for two weeks of rehearsals before shooting began. The only hitch was that all the actors would have to stay in character for the duration of their stay. "We had such a great time," Jennifer recalled. "We got to know each other as our characters. It was a process I hadn't been through with any other director. It went well. And they taught me a thing or two."

The lessons Jennifer learned, especially those about working with such living legends as Coppola, served her well on her next project. Before starting work on *Jack*, Jennifer had been cast in *Blood and Wine*, a family drama/ diamond-heist story starring Jack Nicholson,

Michael Caine, Judy Davis, and Stephen Dorff. Jennifer had endured six auditions with director Bob Rafelson, but she finally won the role of Gabriella, Nicholson's Cuban mistress.

Jennifer will never forget the first time she met Jack Nicholson during a rehearsal. She was sitting next to Michael Caine when Nicholson walked into the room. She still remembers how her heart leaped when the director asked Nicholson to take a seat next to her because their characters were supposed to be romantically involved in the film. With Nicholson on one side and Caine on the other, Jennifer was nearly in shock. "I looked at one and then the other," she recounted. "Then it was like I had an out-of-body experience! I wondered to myself: 'What am I doing in this room with these people?'

Jennifer appears in a scene with Jack Nicholson from the film Blood and Wine. *Jennifer jumped at the chance to act alongside such stars as Nicholson, Michael Caine, and Judy Davis.*

It was very scary. But fun."

Always quick to adapt, Jennifer soon got used to her new surroundings. She did not always hit it off with Nicholson, once calling him a "legend in his own time and in his own mind." She did, however, get on famously with the "really charming" Stephen Dorff, although their relationship never went beyond friendship. Jennifer had found another romantic prospect—someone who had nothing to do with the film industry.

Since *Blood and Wine* was shot in and around the Miami area, Jennifer had lots of chances to savor the regional cuisine. She often visited Larios on the Beach, famous Latina singer Gloria Estefan's Cuban restaurant. Dining frequently at Larios, however, was not a credit to the food alone. Jennifer had fallen head over heels in love with a tall, dark, and handsome model, Ojani Noa, a waiter at the restaurant. Her assistant remembers Jennifer saying "That's the man I'm going to marry" the first time she laid eyes on Noa.

After asking around, Jennifer learned that Noa had been in the United States less than five years. A recent arrival from Cuba, who had fled his native land on a raft, Noa spoke better Spanish than English. Jennifer was embarrassed to approach him because of her rusty Spanish. It could have ended at that, but Jennifer kept returning to Larios. Finally, frustrated with the slow pace of the courtship, one of Jennifer's friends engineered a meeting. The two were a hot item within a matter of weeks.

Although Jennifer was committed to Noa, she was equally determined to pursue her career. When she was offered a major role in *Anaconda*, an action-thriller about gigantic snakes starring Ice Cube, Eric Stoltz, and Jon Voight, Jennifer could not turn it down. With all the makings of a summer blockbuster, the film virtually guaranteed to put her on the map. The producers, however, offered her less money than she had anticipated. Not a person to sell herself short, she asked for more. She knew what she wanted, and she went after it. As she has described it, "When we were negotiating my money . . . I said, 'What? They don't want to give me that? Do they know that I'm going to be wet, bloody, tied up.' I said, 'This is no good. They've got to give me more money.'"

Jennifer took the role, however. After playing a somewhat passive woman in *Blood and Wine*, she was not about to pass up the part of the kind of empowered female she had portrayed in *Money Train*. "I'm the hero," Jennifer enthused to *E!* "I play a first-time documentary director who goes down to the Amazon. She's all excited, but then things start going wrong, and she has to take charge of everything. Me and Ice Cube save the day!"

Opportunity knocked once again soon after Jennifer had begun preparing for this heroic role. While filming *Anaconda* in Brazil, her agent called to tell her she had won the role of Selena, which would begin filming in the summer of 1996. Now Jennifer was on a roll, and it seemed as if there was no end in sight.

5

REACHING NEW HEIGHTS

In 1996, Jennifer was still considered a little-known actress. Despite her sexy role in *Blood and Wine* and her starring role in *Anaconda*, she still had not risen to the top. With *Selena*, all that had changed.

Within days of winning the part of Selena, Jennifer's agent called again. Director Oliver Stone wanted her for his new film, *U-Turn*. Jennifer refused. She had met Stone before, and her first encounter with the lauded director had left her with a negative impression. While still working in television, Jennifer had auditioned for Stone's never-completed film about Panamanian dictator Manuel Noriega. Instead of listening to Jennifer's reading, or giving her so much as a second's glance, Stone walked around the room rearranging furniture and shuffling papers. Jennifer was so infuriated that she swore that she would never again audition for, much less work with, Oliver Stone.

Stone, however, was not so easily put off. He met Jennifer's flat-out refusal with another personal request

---

Jennifer accepts her second ALMA award as Outstanding Actress in a Feature Film for her role in Out of Sight. *Despite the breakup of her marriage and the flack surrounding her outspoken comments, Jennifer never gave up her ambitions or lost confidence in her abilities.*

for an audition, and she relented. As she explained, "Well, he called himself and he wants to make amends. I have the upper hand here because I don't care about this movie. I've got *Selena* and I'm getting a million dollars for it." Jennifer's second audition for Oliver Stone was a resounding success. The two got along like old friends, and according to her agent, the role was as good as hers.

Then actress Sharon Stone entered the picture. Also interested in the role, Sharon Stone was the studio's first choice. Hollywood producers want big names, and Sharon Stone was as big as they came. Jennifer shrugged it off, figuring that since the role was that of an Apache Indian, the studio would change the part for Sharon. Besides, Jennifer was too busy to really care that much. When, in the end, Sharon Stone and the studio could not reach an agreement about the price, Oliver Stone again called Jennifer.

By this time, Jennifer had become very excited by the prospect of working with Sean Penn, Nick Nolte, and Oliver Stone. So she did not hesitate to sign on the dotted line. By the time that shoot wrapped, Jennifer would have done *Blood and Wine*, *Anaconda*, *Selena*, and *U-Turn* all back-to-back.

As Jennifer remembered:

[I]n the beginning, I was really excited with each new project that I was getting, and they all had to be pushed for me to be in them, because one was overlapping the other. The thing was, the movies were good, and the people involved were so good I couldn't turn them down and say, "You know what? I need rest." . . . You can rest later, yes. This was my time to really grab on and say, "Hey, the opportunities are coming. I need to take these."

Looking forward to another long stretch of work on *U-Turn*, Jennifer attended the wrap party for *Selena* with Ojani Noa. To everyone's surprise, he stepped up to the mike, held out a diamond ring, and gave Jennifer something else to look forward to. Before the entire cast, crew, and others at the party, Ojani proposed. Clearly, the couple's relationship had not been derailed by her kamikaze work schedule. With Ojani visiting her on sets and spending his free moments at her side, the two had grown even closer. Jennifer had only to hear the proposal and the wrap party turned into an engagement party. The couple would be married right after Jennifer finished her work on *U-Turn*.

Once filming began, Jennifer was only too happy that she had given Oliver Stone another chance. "He's not crazy, he's a genius," she said. "I love Oliver, loved working with him. He was totally great to me—a real actor's director." Playing the role of Grace McKenna, the troubled Apache woman who cheats on her husband (Nick Nolte) with Sean Penn, also gave Jennifer the opportunity to spend a lot of time with two of her favorite actors. For Jennifer, working with Sean and Nick Nolte, an actor she characterized as "truly amazing," was acting with the best.

The only thing that could top Jennifer's tremendous experience on *U-Turn* was her upcoming wedding to Ojani. The pair decided on February 22, 1997, as their wedding date. With only three months to plan the 200-person

Following her smash performance in Selena, *Jennifer hit the top in Hollywood. With all her fame and popularity, she continued to pursue her goal of becoming a superstar, making as many films as she could fit in. Here, Jennifer portrays an Apache Indian in the film* U-Turn, *which also starred Nick Nolte and Sean Penn.*

affair, Jennifer and Ojani had to pull out all the stops to get everything ready in time for the Miami-based ceremony. A wiz at structuring her days, Jennifer managed to plan her wedding, spend time with Ojani, and go Christmas shopping all at the same time.

That holiday season was a wonderful experience for Jennifer, who finally got to spend some of her hard-earned money on her family. Her mom, Lupe, will never forget the black Cadillac that Jennifer presented to her and David for Christmas. "She blindfolded me and took me out of the house," Lupe recollected, "and when I took off the blindfold there was this beautiful car with a big, red ribbon on it."

Jennifer's newfound wealth was also a boon to her hastily planned, but no less extravagant, wedding. When the big day finally arrived, the event was just as the rising star wanted it. The reception was an elaborate affair, with enough flowers to fill a botanical garden. The whole Lopez family, the Quintanillas, members of the *Selena* cast, Oliver Stone, and many of the young couple's mutual friends had turned out to see Jennifer and Ojani exchange vows. Set at the home of one of Ojani's friends, the Catholic ceremony featured Jennifer's two sisters as bridesmaids. Leslie was already married and teaching music to sixth graders. Younger sister Lynda was now a successful radio disc jockey. Both were as happy as they could be for their beaming sister.

After the wedding, the couple spent a few days visiting friends and family before escaping to honeymoon in Key West, Florida. For Jennifer, the break was long overdue. "We are going to sit on the beach and do nothing," she told a reporter who covered the wedding. It would be the last lazy week that Jennifer would enjoy for a long time.

Immediately upon returning from her honeymoon, Jennifer began promoting the release of *Selena*. When the film opened in theaters across the country, her life changed forever. Magazines clamored to interview her, national talk shows vied with one another to book her, and major record company executives were eager to sign her. In only a few weeks, as *Selena* raked in millions and phenomenal reviews flooded in by the dozens, Jennifer became Hollywood's newest hot commodity.

One of the media's favorite questions was about Jennifer's figure. Her figure-revealing costumes in *Selena* revealed more curves than most actresses and fueled a great deal of talk. Her look challenged the view of the super-thin Hollywood actress and even became something of a political statement. In interviews, Jennifer was bombarded with questions about how she felt about being full-figured. Jennifer had absolutely no problem thinking up an appropriate response. "I don't have to be a size 2 to be sexy," she told *Details*. "I love my butt and I was never ashamed of it, and I guess not being ashamed of something like that, which is uncharacteristic of this society, made it become a focal point."

It wasn't until she reached the tabloids that Jennifer realized she had arrived. Various publications, including the Spanish press, printed reports that Jennifer had split with Ojani. Among the tabloids' fabrications were tales of Ojani throwing things at Jennifer, their separation, and his demands for money. Jennifer was outraged. "I was like, 'Where do these people get these stories from?'" she told a reporter. "My husband's mother actually called from Cuba, where they don't even get news all the time, saying, 'What happened? Are you guys getting a divorce?'"

The couple had only just been married and had no intention of divorcing. *Selena* was a hit, and *Anaconda* was well on its way to grossing more than $100 million in worldwide ticket sales. Jennifer was a one-woman publicity

A smiling husband and wife, Jennifer and Ojani Noa share the spotlight at the premiere of Selena. Despite her hectic schedule, Jennifer had organized a lavish wedding, which attracted many of Hollywood's elite.

FHM magazine readers selected Jennifer as "The Sexiest Woman in the World." Despite the accolade, she had reached her goal as an actress who does not have to play only Latina roles and is not just a sexy performer. Her successes also made her the highest-paid Latina actress in Hollywood.

machine, flying from Los Angeles to New York to Miami and back again. Soon, a new film role was in the works.

For Jennifer, making four movies was not a difficult decision. She wanted to strike while the iron was hot, and she got her chance when her agent told her about *Out of Sight*. With George Clooney set to star and Steven Soderbergh to direct, the screen adaptation of the Elmore Leonard novel was just the type of high-class project Jennifer had in mind when she first began her acting career.

Although Sandra Bullock had originally been up for the part, she did not wish to do a screen test. Instead of trying to cajole Bullock, her agent, who was also Jennifer's agent, advised Jennifer to test for the role. The screen test was very important to George Clooney. He had starred opposite such legendary Hollywood beauties as Michelle Pfeiffer and Nicole Kidman without seeming to connect onscreen with any of them. Whoever got the female lead in the film would have to be more than a stunner. She would have to radiate sex appeal and have great chemistry with Clooney.

According to director Soderbergh, Jennifer was the obvious choice for the role of Karen Sisco, the federal marshal who pursues and falls in love with Clooney's prison escapee character, not because viewers were ready to see a Latina actress on the big screen but because viewers were ready to see Jennifer in high-profile films. For her part, Jennifer was thrilled to tackle the role. Her sole stipulation was that she receive a fair fee for her work. Five million dollars was Jennifer's magic number, but the studio thought it could get her for a million. That was unacceptable, and Jennifer persisted, fighting for what she felt was her due.

Jennifer's determined spirit finally landed her a $2 million paycheck. Once again, she had broken records and remained the highest paid Hispanic actress in Hollywood. Just being Hollywood's top Latina was not Jennifer's goal, however. She intended to become a very highly paid actress, Latina or not.

The role of Karen Sisco played a significant part in furthering Jennifer's career. She starred opposite *People* magazine's "Sexiest Man Alive." And since the role did not exploit her as a Latina, Jennifer was simply an actress, not a symbol. "Hollywood is being more open-minded about casting," Jennifer told an interviewer. "I'm perceived as an actress who is Latin—not a Latin actress as in one who just does Latin roles. I'm considered for roles that are not Latin, and that's been a big step in the right direction for me."

Another important step occurred in December 1997. While filming *Out of Sight*, Jennifer finally received public acclaim for her acting. The Golden Globe Awards nominated her for Best Actress in a Comedy or Musical for *Selena*. With Julia Roberts and Helen Hunt among her competition, Jennifer knew that she was slowly but surely inching her way onto Hollywood's elite A list of top stars. Although the trophy ultimately went to Helen Hunt, simply being nominated bolstered Jennifer's status with the establishment. She knew she had been accepted when the following year she was asked to be a presenter at the 1998 Academy Awards. With the impending release of *Out of Sight*, her star showed no signs of dimming. Jennifer seemed to have everything a young woman could dream of.

But all was not smooth sailing for this suddenly famous star. The first sign of trouble in the Lopez paradise erupted from an interview that appeared in the February 1998 issue of *Movieline* magazine. She spoke candidly, giving her honest opinions on the acting abilities of contemporaries such as Cameron Diaz, whom she described as "A lucky model who's been given a lot of opportunities I just wish she would have done more with," and the popular Gwyneth Paltrow, whose talent she dismissed with "Some people get hot by

Jennifer shares a smile with leading man George Clooney, her costar in the film Out of Sight. *Like Jennifer, Clooney can also be outspoken about Hollywood, and he defended her unflattering, highly publicized remarks about other performers.*

association." (She was referring to Paltrow's relationship with actor Brad Pitt.) Winona Ryder, Selma Hayek, Claire Danes, and even her childhood idol Madonna fell victim to Jennifer's biting words.

Jennifer did not think she was being spiteful, however. She was simply saying what she really thought—but the result was near-disaster. Horrified by the article's depiction of her words, Jennifer immediately sent letters of apology to the offended parties. "I didn't want those girls to think I was trying to trash them or anything," she explained. "And I was sorry about the way it came off, I really was, I really lost sleep over it, so I wanted them to know that."

According to George Clooney, Jennifer's remarks had been an honest mistake. "We all do 'em," he commented. "There should really be someone who gives you lessons about fame and teaches you what to say and what not to do. . . . She had to battle after the *Movieline* incident and it was really fun to be around her then because she's a real fighter." The flap over the article would eventually die down, but it was not the worst of Jennifer's problems.

She was in the midst of a divorce from Ojani. Her husband was constantly upset over Jennifer's love scenes, revealing dresses, and hefty paychecks. Stressed and uncomfortable in her marriage, Jennifer had to make a simple choice: Ojani or her career. As Ojani put it to the *New York Post*, "She wanted her career, so everything with us went out the window."

As much as Jennifer had wanted her marriage to work, she knew she had rushed into it prematurely. She acknowledged that she was young and naïve and thought that love was all that mattered in a marriage. Of the breakup she commented, ". . . you have to compromise to a certain extent. Sometimes people are just not ready to do that at that point in their lives." After little more than a year of marriage, the couple went their separate ways. Neither felt ill will, only sadness, and they have remained friends and still speak on occasion.

For all that she learned from her bitter

experience, the spring of 1998 was not the best time for Jennifer Lopez. Her personal life had fallen apart, and the _Movieline_ article had cast a pall over her acting career. Jennifer needed to do something drastic to boost her flagging spirits. Not one to sit around feeling sorry for herself, Jennifer decided to sink all her energy into fulfilling an old dream: making music.

QUEEN OF ALL MEDIA

F ew ever suspected that Jennifer Lopez had a secret weapon. When she unleashed her hidden talent upon the world, however, it was clear that international superstardom was her's for the taking. Playing the role of a singer in *Selena* had reminded Jennifer how much she had enjoyed performing live in the past. She remembered the singing, dancing, and applause, and she wanted them back. When her career hit a small snag in 1998, she decided there was no time like the present. "I cut a demo all in Spanish," she explained, "but the big companies were more interested in doing an English record. So I decided the record would be a blend of all of my influences." For inspiration she looked to performers like Barbra Streisand, Cher, Diana Ross, and Bette Midler.

One of the big companies that Jennifer approached was Sony Music. When its chief, Tommy Mottola, listened to Jennifer's demo tape, he wasted no time before picking up the phone. Jeff Ayeroff, copresident of Sony's Work Group label, was just as quick to champion Jennifer's

This is a publicity photograph of Jennifer that was released to promote her debut album, On the 6. *With this smash recording and the top singles she produced as a singer, Jennifer proved that she could conquer the music world as well as the film world.*

determination to shine in the music industry. He signed Jennifer the first time he met her.

Although a novice recording artist, Jennifer knew exactly what she wanted in her debut album, *On the 6*. (The title is a reference to the Number 6 train she took as a young girl from the Bronx to Manhattan for dancing classes.) Taking a hands-on approach to every aspect of production, she listened to songs by artists ranging from Babyface to Diane Warren. In the end, however, Jennifer decided that her record would be a reflection of her roots. "I felt it was important," she said, "that my record be less pop and have more urban Latin appeal."

Spending the second half of 1998 and the first few months of 1999 shuttling between recording studios and hotel rooms in New York, Los Angeles, and Miami, Jennifer limited her film work to voicing the part of Azteca in the animated smash *Antz*, and concentrated primarily on her album. When the producers encouraged her to write some songs for the album, she created the haunting ballad "Should Have Never," a song about a woman who loses control of her life when she meets a man. Many speculated it reflects her failed marriage with Ojani, but Jennifer denies that rumor. She also cowrote two other songs and recorded a Spanish-language duet with Latino star Marc Anthony entitled "You Must Not Love Me."

Although Jennifer was practically locked away in the studio, her public image was fast becoming that of the sexiest woman alive. Following the release of *Out of Sight*, she took on endorsements for Coca-Cola and nabbed a highly paid contract with L'Oreal hair products and cosmetics. At the same time, rumors were circulating about the identity of her latest boyfriend, including gossip that she was romantically involved with Sony Music's Tommy Mottola. Both Jennifer and Mottola hotly denied anything between them but friendship. Columnists were also busy churning out stories of a relationship with rapper and hip-hop impresario Sean "Puffy" Combs. Although Jennifer had no comments about Combs, he had put her on the cover of his multicultural magazine, *Notorious*, and had also written and produced a track on her album. With all the publicity, the stage was set for the release of Jennifer's first single.

In the spring of 1999, Jennifer exploded on to the music scene with her first single, "If You Had My Love." Featuring Jennifer's slinky, sexy dancing, the accompanying video was an instant hit with the MTV crowd. Soon the single even overtook Ricky Martin's "Livin' La Vida Loca" to become number one on *Billboard's* Hot 100 list for five straight weeks.

On the 6, however, was not the quick money maker that Sony had hoped for, but it did have something going for it that many other new releases did not—a long shelf life. After turning out another single, "Waiting for Tonight," and watching it climb the charts, Jennifer could finally breathe a sigh of relief. Thanks to her heavily rotated singles and videos, *On the 6* went double platinum within 10 months of its release.

As a newly arrived singer, Jennifer suddenly found her appearance schedule very full. In addition to promoting her album, she was in constant demand to perform at a variety of events. She entertained spectators at the start of the 1999 Women's World Cup in Pasadena,

With her soaring popularity, Jennifer was in constant demand to appear at all kinds of events. Here she energizes the crowd at the 1999 Women's World Cup soccer game in the Rose Bowl in Pasadena, California.

California, and proudly served as National Grand Marshal in New York City's Puerto Rican Day Parade. On December 5 she performed at the VH-1 Fashion Awards in New York City, and three days later she wowed the audience at the Billboard Music Awards in Las Vegas. Jennifer was also besieged by invitations from the MTV Video Music Awards, the American Music Awards, and the Grammys.

She was not only invited to these awards ceremonies, however. Having already won nominations and trophies for her work in *Selena*, Jennifer garnered further accolades. The VH-1 Fashion Awards named her Most Fashionable Female Artist of 1999, and she celebrated the new millennium by winning the prestigious ALMA award, Female Entertainer of the Year. An award Jennifer especially prizes is the 1999 Teen Choice Award for Song of the Summer, "If You Had My Love." The video that accompanied this single earned Jennifer four MTV Music Video Awards nominations.

With one foot planted firmly in the music world, Jennifer kept the other grounded in Hollywood by taking on a new film role. She signed on for top billing in *The Cell*, a psychological thriller that also starred Vince Vaughn. Cast in the role of a scientist, Jennifer more than doubled her asking price by demanding—and receiving—$5 million for her work. Soon thereafter, she was slated to play the title role in *The Wedding Planner*, a romantic comedy also starring heartthrob Brendan Fraser. Proof of her rise to superstardom is that she can now command $9 million a film.

On the downside, a young woman with such phenomenal success and power simply could not hide from the pressures of fame. Her manager, Benny Medina, explains: "I think there's a tremendous fascination with Jennifer. When she goes somewhere and there are other celebrities, she's the one the [photographers] flock to. She can't go anywhere anymore without being mobbed." With such frenzied attention, it is almost impossible for Jennifer to hide her personal life, especially her romantic involvements.

After months of denying the rumors that she and Puffy Combs were an item, the couple finally decided to come out of hiding in the fall of 1999. Soon after they had begun appearing together in public, an incident in New York City made headlines in the media.

On December 26, 1999, Puffy and Jennifer were allegedly involved in a shooting in a nightclub in midtown Manhattan. Reportedly, when Puffy tried to impress the patrons by tossing around money, one customer flung it back to him. Immediately, Puffy's friend, a rapper named Shyne, pulled out a gun and started shooting. By the time the police arrived, Jennifer and Puffy had made the mistake of fleeing the scene. After running 10 red lights, their car was pulled over and they were arrested when police found what was believed to be a stolen gun in the car. What followed was like a scene from a movie. Jennifer was handcuffed to a bench and detained in a holding cell for some 14 hours. She was finally released, and all charges against her were dropped. Although protesting his innocence, Puffy was charged with criminal possession of a weapon and possessing stolen property.

Jennifer's love, Sean "Puffy" Combs gives her a hug and a kiss. Despite the notoriety of the shooting incident in New York City, Jennifer refused to leave Combs, declaring her love for him.

Many thought Jennifer should leave Puffy then and there. She was in love, however, and she remained loyal to Puffy, always maintaining his innocence. "Jennifer is standing by her man," said Uptown Records founder Andre Harrell, "and as a friend of Puffy's, I can honestly say that I have seen the loving way they look at each other when they're in a room together." Other friends have noted how much the two have in common, including their age, their roots, and especially their determination to be at the top.

When she has time off from her crowded schedule and is not fending off the press, Jennifer relaxes at her home in West Hollywood, which she shares with her cocker spaniel, Boots. She also enjoys breezing around the town in her Mercedes convertible. As for the famous figure that has so captivated the public, she keeps it in shape. Jennifer works out four times a week and only eats egg whites before noon. She neither smokes, drinks, nor indulges in drugs. "I work really hard to have my body the way it is," she told *Elle* magazine.

While Jennifer lives in Hollywood, she considers the Bronx her real home and often visits her old neighborhood. Her parents still live there, and her mother still teaches at the Holy Family School. Lupe is justly proud of her famous daughter, and in her classroom proudly displays a poster advertising the film *Selena*, along with a photograph of Jennifer with President Bill Clinton. On her visits, Jennifer often appears at schools, speaking to students about getting an education and pursuing their dreams.

As for her reputation as a "diva," a characterization that in Hollywood generally means an actress is difficult and arrogant, Jennifer has admitted that she has a problem with the term. "I feel like it means that you are mean to people, that you look down on people, and I'm not that type of person." At the same time, she knows she is ambitious, and she is confident of her worth. "Just because I know my strengths doesn't mean I have a huge ego," she explains. "When it comes to my work, I am

an ogre, because I want it to be so good . . .
I don't want people bothering me. I need my
time. But that's the only thing anyone can say
about me."

Taking chances, whether in love or in her
career, has been Jennifer Lopez's main strategy
for success. From dancing on television to starring in films and music, Jennifer has always
been willing to take risks. "The winners take
risks," she has said. "That's the only way to be."

While no one can guess what's next for this
talented singer, dancer, and actress, the only
certainty is that Jennifer will be around to
keep fans guessing for many years to come.

CHRONOLOGY

1970   Born on July 24 in the Bronx, New York.

1977   Begins dance classes.

1987   Graduates from high school; drops out of New York's Baruch College to pursue dance on a full-time basis.

1991   Chosen to be a Fly Girl on Fox TV's *In Living Color*; moves to Los Angeles.

1993   Quits *In Living Color* to appear in the short-lived Fox TV series *South Central* and *Second Chances*.

1994   Appears in TV series *Hotel Malibu*.

1995   Films TV movie *Nurses on the Line: The Crash of Flight 7*; makes feature film debut in Gregory Nava's *My Family/Mi Familia*; films *The Money Train*.

1996   Plays a supporting role in the film *Jack*.

1997   Stars in *Blood and Wine, Anaconda, Selena*, and *U-Turn*; becomes the highest-paid Latina actress in Hollywood; nominated for a Golden Globe Award as Best Actress in a Comedy or Musical category for *Selena*; marries Ojani Noa.

1998   Stars in *Out of Sight* with George Clooney; *Antz* is released; signs a recording contract with Sony Records; divorces Ojani Noa.

1999   Releases debut album, *On the 6*; first single, "If You Had My Love," remains No. 1 on *Billboard*'s Hot 100 list for five straight weeks; *On the 6* goes platinum; begins dating Sean "Puffy" Combs.

2000   *On the 6* goes double platinum; wins ALMA Award for Female Entertainer of the Year; *The Cell* is released.

2001   Breaks up with Sean "Puffy" Combs; *The Wedding Planner* released; *Angel Eyes* released; *J. Lo*, her follow-up album to *On the 6* released; marries Cris Judd, a dancer and choreographer, on September 29 in California.

ACCOMPLISHMENTS

Television

1991   *In Living Color*

1993   *Second Chances*
              South Central

1994   *Hotel Malibu*

1995   *Nurses on the Line: The Crash of Flight 7*

Films

1995   *My Family/Mi Familia*
              Money Train

1996   *Jack*

1997   *Blood and Wine*
              Selena
              Anaconda
              U-Turn

1998   *Out of Sight*
              Antz (voice)

2000   *The Cell*

2001   *The Wedding Planner*
              Angel Eyes

Discography

1999   *On the 6*

2001   *J. Lo*
              "What's Going On" (an ensemble single/album to benefit the
              United Way's September 11th Fund and the AIDS relief effort)

AWARDS

1998   ALMA Award for Best Actress for *Selena*; Lasting Image Award for *Selena*; Lone Star Film and Television Award for Best Actress for *Selena*

1999   ALMA Award for Outstanding Actress in a Feature Film for *Out of Sight*; Teen Choice Award for Song of the Summer ("If You Had My Love"); VH-1 Fashion Award for Most Fashionable Female Artist

2000   ALMA Awards for Female Entertainer of the Year and Outstanding Music Video Performer; MTV Music Award for Best Dance Video

FURTHER READING

Cortina, Betty, and Pam Lambert. "Viva Selena!" *People*, March 1997.

Degen, Pener. "From Here to Divinity: With Role Models Like Babs, Bette, and Cher, Does Divalicious Jennifer Lopez Aspire To Be the New Miss Thang?" *Entertainment Weekly*, October 1998.

Duncan, Patricia. *Jennifer Lopez*. New York: St. Martin's Press, 1999.

Frankel, Marha. "Love in Bloom." *In Style*, May 1997.

Hill, Anne E. *Jennifer Lopez*. Philadelphia: Chelsea House Publishers, 2000.

Johns, Michael-Anne. *Jennifer Lopez*. Kansas City, Mo.: Andrews McMeel Publishing, 2000.

———. "Casting Presents Challenges for 'Selena' Filmmakers." *El Sol Del Valle*, April 3, 1997.

INDEX

ALMA Award, 12, 55

Anaconda (film), 8, 34-35, 37, 38, 42

Anthony, Marc, 52

Antz (film; voice), 52

Ayeroff, Jeff, 51-52

Billboard Music Awards, 55

Blood and Wine (film), 32-34, 35, 37, 38

Carrey, Jim, 25, 28

Cell, The (film), 55

Clooney, George, 44, 45, 48

Combs, Sean "Puffy" (boyfriend), 53, 56-58

Coppola, Francis Ford, 32

Cruz, David (ex-boyfriend), 18-19, 27, 30-31

Danes, Claire, 47

Diaz, Cameron, 46

Dorff, Stephen, 33, 34

Golden Musicals of Broadway, The (variety show), 23

Gold, Eric, 25, 28

Harrell, Andre, 57

Hayek, Selma, 47

Hotel Malibu (TV), 28

"If You Had My Love" (single), 13, 53, 55

In Living Color (TV), 25, 27, 28

Jack (film), 32

Lopez, David (father), 15-16, 22

Lopez, Guadalupe "Lupe" (mother), 15-16, 17, 18-19, 22, 40-41, 58

Lopez, Jennifer
  appearance of, 42
  awards received by, 12, 55
  birth of, 15
  childhood of, 15-18
  and dancing, 10, 11, 16, 19, 21-25, 27
  divorce of, 48-49
  education of, 16, 18, 21, 22
  and endorsements, 52
  family of, 15-19
  and leisure activities, 58
  marriage of.
    See Noa, Ojani

Lopez, Leslie (sister), 15, 16-17, 22, 41

Lopez, Lynda (sister), 15, 16-17, 41

Madonna, 47

Medina, Benny, 56

Money Train (film), 30, 31-32, 35

Moreno, Rita, 17-18

Mottola, Tommy, 51, 53

MTV Movie Award, 12

My Family/Mi Familia (film), 10, 28-29, 32

Nava, Gregory, 9-10, 28, 29

Nicholson, Jack, 32, 33-34

Noa, Ojani (ex-husband), 34, 39-41, 42, 48, 52

Nolte, Nick, 38, 39

Nurses on the Line: The Crash of Flight 7 (TV), 28

On the 6 (album), 13, 52, 53

Out of Sight (film), 12, 44-46, 52

Paltrow, Gwyneth, 46-47

Penn, Sean, 38, 39

Puerto Rican Day Parade, 55

Quintanilla, Abraham, Jr., 9

Rafelson, Bob, 33

Ryder, Winona, 47

Second Chances (TV), 28

Selena (film), 7-12, 13, 35, 37, 38, 39, 41-42, 51, 58

Soderbergh, Steven, 44, 45

Sony Music, 51-52

South Central (TV), 28

Stone, Oliver, 37-38, 39, 41

Stone, Sharon, 38

Teen Choice Award, 55

U-Turn (film), 37-39

VH-1 Fashion Awards, 55

"Waiting for Tonight" (single), 53

Wedding Planner, The (film), 55

West Side Story, 17-18

Women's World Cup, 53

ABOUT THE AUTHOR

LEAH FURMAN is a freelance writer living in New York City. The author of more than 20 books, her biographies include *Heart of Soul: The Lauryn Hill Story*, *Happily Ever After: The Drew Barrymore Story*, *Korn: Life in the Pit*, *Give It to You: The Jordan Knight Story*, *Rumours Exposed: The Story of Fleetwood Mac*, and *Enrique Iglesias*. Her other titles include *The Everything Dating Book*, *Generation Inc: Best Business Bets for Young Entrepreneurs*, and *The Everything After College Book*.